Ornithomancy

Ornithomancy

Poems

Mollie Jackman

Ornithomancy
©2022 Mollie Jackman

Kaleidoscope first appeared in Coffin Bell Journal, Volume 3, Issue No. 3

Published by Off & Running Publications
OffandRunningPublications.com

Paperback ISBN: 979-8-9895038-0-3
ebook ISBN: 979-8-9895038-1-0

Cover design by Youssef Abdalla
Illustrations by Maggie Jackman
Interior design by Liz Schreiter

O|R

For Sharon Schertel and Wendy Dwyer,
who introduced me to poems.

Thank you to Maggie and Youssef, for lending
your visions to this book. To all the artists who
helped bring it to life. To my friends and family
for your stories and support.

Prayer for a Poet

May it come in dreams
  and fuel your nightmares

The most enchanting flower
  in The Alnwick Garden

May your words be antidotes
  for the petals' poison

May you write it better,
  or far, far worse

Unfurl with hope, or
  stand, and root with fear

May your worry overcome,
  become illuminated manuscript

Florid first-editions scrawled
  in parking lots, on receipt paper

A prayer to Apollo, Saint Sylvia,
  whoever will listen;

May you find old Edgar
  on his park bench

Some dark corner of the Underland

Contents

Reader,

As I write this, I can't quite picture you in my mind. Are you thumbing through this copy in a library aisle? Sitting on a park bench, reading through the din of children on the playground? In an old armchair by a cozy fire, at a window seat commuting home from work… I could go on, but the point is, I hope you read this book everywhere.

For so long, poems have been relegated to the smallest section of the bookstore, to the highly academic audience, to MFAs and fellow poets. But it's time for a new era. Poetry is not reserved for beatniks and hipsters in New York lofts with exposed brick. It's not just here to serve angsty artists (though we do love it), and you don't need a SparkNotes guide to enjoy it. In fact, if this is your first time reading a poetry book, I have some advice: stop trying to read it "right." That's the special thing about poetry; it can move us in ways we don't yet understand. Maybe that line you loved will make sense by the end, and maybe it won't. But stay in the moment and keep reading.

Prayer for a Poet asks for inspiration, but the poem's wish for the reader is simply to feel. The Alnwick Poison Garden is a deadly attraction in the UK filled with a hundred breathtaking but poisonous plants. Apollo was the Greek god of plague, but also healing, poetry, and music. Beauty doesn't come without struggle. And it doesn't require a complex knowledge of art to understand that.

Ornithomancy took its inspiration from the hardest years of my life. These poems carried me through loss and darkness in a way that only they could. Some of them poured out of me like the songs programmed into those 90's keyboards, pre-programmed with "My Heart Will Go On." Others took more excavating than I've ever had to do.

Friends shared the weirdest stories they'd ever heard, mythology from around the world offered up reimagined viewpoints. Dreams materialized onto the page, and tragedy did the same. This book helped me through my hardest times, and I hope it can do the same for you.

See you next time,
Mollie

Katabasis

noun: a going or marching down or back

Start at your childhood home.
Pack a bindleful of peaches.
Later, eat them with the skin on—
fuzz like velvet on your tongue,
palms, sticky with nectar.
Beyond the back yard
touch the tops of tall grass
with your sugary hands,
hear it whistle, softly as you go.

The Alien Cave is an old concrete drainpipe,
transformed with graffiti
a few concrete posts in the middle—
you perch on them, wait to be
beamed into anywhere

Run home—cross the fallen log, just like a movie
Grip tight the tree lined high with poison ivy.
Later we'll hide in the master bath,
clean the toxins from our skin
with your mother's best laundry.
Remember?
At 17, suspend your disbelief
to search for Griffons in Washington woods.
Later, at your dinner table,
hear your brother talk of River Osprey.

Angel of the Used Car Dealer

A group of six-year-olds sit
huddled in a bay window
their sleeping bags, sparking with static
when they see her spotlight
lighting up the sky

They wonder if some aliens
have come to take them
in the night, but someone
pulls a silver cross
from under her extra-large t-shirt
and whispers it's an angel
as it starts to snow

Missouri's oldest Bur Oak, "The Big Tree" in McBaine, MO

Excerpt from *Journal of the Siam Society*
Written by Suchitra Chongstitvatana

"In Thai literary tradition the term 'Nirat' is clearly associated with a kind of love poem—a lamentation of love when the poet is on a journey and separated from <their> beloved. The essence of the Nirat lies in the charm of the expression of longing and desire in the descriptions of places and people."

Floodwater
Nirat to The Big Tree, Columbia MO

June 7, 2019.

It's early evening, but Missouri sun still peeks through my southward windows. The front garden glistens with hosewater—but miles away, the fields are brimming. The Muddy Tributary rolls like the tops of the wheat fields it's flooded. Water spreads like soybeans through the fertile ground.

Somehow, the water makes the Bur Oak bigger—the only landmark in a vast expanse of misplaced river. They ride past on jet skis; little wakes wash towards its massive trunk. I see myself there, or Brittany and I, underwater.

May 10, 2019.

I cross into Ohio after a 7-hour solo road trip and the farms have transformed. The state I came from is full of corn, dotted here and there with a dilapidated, leaning old barn. Wood rots and vultures make nests in their hay lofts. I traversed the Mississippi this morning, all the silos, half-submerged. It's different here. Picket fences border landscaped farmhouses; pink pampas frames their barn-doors and orange wildflowers warm their crop fields. Barn swallows flit over their roofs. There is no barbed wire in sight. No flood-plain danger. I wonder if this place is anything like the one you flew home from. I picture us sitting in your living room, looking at your photos on some old projector.

October 9, 2018.

It's morning outside Boone County Courthouse. I'm holding some papers in my hands, sitting on an old blue Subaru, new to me, playing out the next few hours in my mind. The sun lights Broadway as though through polarized lenses. The city feels sharp—a vision, or a bed of tacks.

I cross the street and walk into the courtroom. I don't cry in front of the judge. I don't tell him what happened. I just accept a traffic fine and stop for coffee on the way to the office.

September 1, 2018.

It's 3pm. I took a weird way home with a carful of groceries, and the August sun is somewhere. I see a gray Toyota truck—like yours, with the little bed. After a second, I remember you're dead, and a second after that I hear my hood crunch like a black accordion, and "Chad Johnson's" plastic license plate holder is cracked. And "Officer Bieber" says "I'm sure you were expecting this," and hands me a citation with a court date. Then he makes me give it back, scratches it out, and writes a new one. They all drive away as I pick the eggs up off my floorboard.

August 31, 2018.

It's dark already when I arrive. Your memorial service has a cash bar, and Naif tries to pay with his vacation-currency and we laugh, a lot. I hug Brittany. There are so many photos. Board games at every table, bruschetta and fancy meatballs on trays. People tell stories and someone sings a song they wrote, based on your favorite "Office" quote.

"I wish there was a way to know you're in the good old days, before you've actually left them."

There's a tearful rendition of Piano Man. Brittany hugs me. I go outside, sit on a bench in front of the Alumni Center, stare at Jesse Hall. I ask the universe to tell me when it's time to go home, and a light on the fire escape flickers on. In the parking garage, the rows light up as I walk under.

August 27, 2018.

It's exactly sunset when I arrive at the Big Tree. A procession of cars leaving, there's a lone soul left under its canopy. Long blonde hair aglow in the pink and yellow. And it's Brittany. Astonished, we laugh and say we both came here for "Nathan Time." You brought her here once, a roommate bonding day. I came alone, many nights. We talk about birds, and the number twenty-seven: the day we've found each other here, a wrong-turn bike ride realized at mile 13.5, a record you two bought together. The age I turned the day you left us. We sat there til the last of sun was gone, floodwater rising up in us.

August 23, 2018.

I was born at 11:01, twenty-seven years ago today; mid-day at a little hospital, just off the St. Charles riverbank in mid-Missouri. Today I leave work early, make myself pretty, and return a call on the way to dinner. "Did you know Nathan?" she asks on the other end, past tense.

I did.

You texted me at 3am, from a terminal, halfway across the world. *Happy Birthday!* you said, *I can't wait to show you the pictures.*

Excerpt from the Columbia Missourian, Feb. 1, 2016

Columbia man gets probation for throwing rocks at vehicles, injuring woman

Written by Jack Waddell

COLUMBIA — A man who pleaded guilty to assault and property damage in connection with throwing rocks at vehicles on Stadium Boulevard was given a suspended sentence Monday of five years' probation...

According to the probable cause statement, ███████ walked across Stadium Boulevard about 5 p.m. on Nov. 1, 2014, picked up some large rocks on the side of the road and began throwing them at parked vehicles...

███████ then began throwing rocks at cars traveling on Stadium Boulevard and damaged the windshields of two of them. One passenger was struck in the face and had to be hospitalized for head injuries, including a concussion and an orbital socket fracture. Five children in the same vehicle were also struck by glass...

...███████ was intoxicated and he has since sought counseling.

███████ also has to pay restitution of $4,246.62 to the woman who was injured and whose car was damaged in the incident.

Bang

It starts with a rock
in the hand of a teenage boy, or

two asteroids dancing
around each other.

In space, or the hollow, where
he'll keep this moment
a black hole, or a universe.

The asteroids spin closer
getting dizzy

and he wanders to the shoulder,
aimless fist around a piece
of limestone.

Spinning, spinning, stardust
settled long ago
is stirring

he raises his stone
like a baseball, and lets it
fly.
When the asteroids collide, there's glitter
everywhere—the Universe ascends
into existence

where the baseball rock has clambered
out of young hands
into windshield
and orbital socket

And the dark red blood of
a mother, in the passenger seat
of the minivan, is pooling
in the eye that she will
not see from, again—

a universe, or
a black hole.

The Phoenix

The Phoenix is trying to burn us down. We douse the churches, restore them to their former glory while the temples return to the Earth as ash. The born again refuse to be reincarnated. Notre Dame refuses to be consumed.

The redwoods go up and they come down hard. A thunderous impact, drowned out by the sea of surrounding flames. A smoky pillar rises from the embers.

Dead things litter the former forest floor. A funeral pyre of old foliage.

The Phoenix spreads its fiery wings and lights savannah grass ablaze. The god-bird warns it's time to start again.

Artemis

A single arrow
into misty morning.
He thinks he misses.
All goes quiet, for just a moment

then,

her form comes crashing
brown leaves, a partition
almost hiding
the blood.

She thrashes closer, and he sees them;
two front legs, barely
hanging.

So he follows her down
to the creek bed, takes
a deep breath—
his next release,
her lungs. It won't be long, now.

He sits beside her
on wet creek rocks,
plants himself to stay until
her last warm doe-breath
whispers into cold.

Ode to Funeral Homes

Honey roasted peanuts in the basement
on the thin, red patterned carpet
and the sound of tornado sirens

A man walked to the podium
opened a binder
broke into song

I tucked a poem in a satin pocket
of your casket–roses were
red, violets were blue, I love you, something something.

In the high school cafeteria
the night you died we passed
a box of tissues, buried hatchets, time

The smell of hotel breakfast–maple syrup, bitter coffee
wafting through the elevator door, we load our bags
into the car, go
on

Migrations

A full moon tonight
but no bird in the sky
for 100 miles

no hawk
on his fencepost
to bid us safe travels

And I wonder if the absence of the avian
is ominous as endless 'possums
littering the eastbound freeway

some laid on their backs
tongues out, arms reaching
as if for something –

others, ghosts of former selves,
spill out onto the interstate
in pleading - we need to mean something

The way home will be warded
with a dozen v's of
Branta Canadensis

For luck,
the correspondence says,
but they don't feel lucky

Night

I watch a fleshless talon
flex its bone-white tendons,
scrape my still chest
pulling me–

a hooked fish, just
come down through the surface
breathe some of your air bubbles
into the stillness

In a blink, this Gone God's grasp has vanished
I click on the lamp and my nightstand
is covered–black soot
from some unearthly furnace

Memoriam

Death creeps through my dreams of you
like early frost through a morning garden
and I wonder
if I'd gone to the funeral

Would your still face haunt me
like the smiling one does?

Then death is a snake and,
I am mother rabbit.
Each night watching little long-ears
romp in tall grass, unseeing the long S
nearer by the second.
Tomorrow, at the slightest rustle
I will call them home.

Clathrus Archeri or Octopus Stinkhorn mushroom

Anatomy of the In-Between

Sometimes the two worlds meet like
oil and water—tiny droplets, viscerally
float, submerge, disperse to memory

Like that half a Red-Eared Slider in the garden
marked by some hungry canine's crescent
shaped like death—but from the
left, he still looked living

Or the Dead-Bird-Box Turtle
we stopped to move
but walked up to the center line
to find his shell was feathers
head, a bent bird's neck
stretching into forever

Or the mushroom carcass—
bony ribcage blooming from decay
I'd swear it was an animal, except for
those roots

I whisper into them, and listen
for an answer
from some empty tin can
on the other side

Shadows dance in Plato's Allegory of the Cave

An Open Letter from Plato's Cave

after Plato's Allegory of the Cave

When you left the darkness
I was sad for you
our shadow puppets
grieved your empty
space and I can feel
a breeze, now
to the left of me
you used to sit there
then you got smaller
and brighter, and farther
and I can never see you anymore

Once, a strange pale creature came
and he used your voice
and he talked of another
a place that's strange and beautiful
with nothing we've ever seen
before—but I closed my eyes
so tight and this wild apparition
went down with the sun
and I feel so very much
alive here—I am not
giving in
to the light

Golden Hour

Sleek summer bluebirds rustle up
roadside—wet and gold
with last drops of sunlight

It hangs on the trees like a snowdrift,
last of daytime,
finally falls, a flash on horizon

the moon starts to rise
from the highway

The Knowing

When Kayla died I dreamed I saw her again.
In a halfway house, somewhere between here and heaven.
In a room with a cot and a door that won't shut
all the way—her eyes, glassed over.

"They made me cut my hair," she whispered
and I remember
her with purple dreadlocks, unlaced high tops
cigarette behind her ear.

She wonders if the halfway house is heaven.
She wonders if it isn't,
then how do we get there?
She wonders if I am dead, too.

I wake on a twin bed,
in my teenage bedroom
posters removed but the holes from their thumbtacks
confirm my existence.

The night that my grandpa died
my mother slept here—
she tells me that she sat with him
replayed their lives together
She stayed up with his spirit
til she couldn't any longer; she said

"Dad, I think I need to go to sleep now"
and she heard him close the front door on his way home.

"He's OK now," she tells me
as I recount my dream this morning
"He's OK now."
And she calls it The Knowing.

Carbon, as an Old Man to his Grandchildren

Dark, the day that I was born and light,
as sudden as a car crash but
smaller

Now they build me coliseums
great holes in the Earth
to find me, shining
after lifetimes
in the Underland

they'll burn me
and breathe me
ink me into their skin
an eternity
of consumption
just to bury me again

Treehouse

"This property," my mother says, "has something special."
We sit in the treehouse and watch the dappled moonlight
filter through the trees.
There used to be more of them, when I was young,
but the elders that remain are taller than our home by three
times over.

The yard has evolved in other ways, still.

A mesh inlay braces the old sledding hill from erosion,
black snakes often get stuck in the netting, easy prey for
stalking hawks and Barn Owls
so my father takes a pair of kitchen scissors, cuts them out,
and sets them back into the brush.
He creates a bridge of an old cobwebbed broom, to encourage
the family of raccoons
to move out of his garden shed.

When they tore down the walls in the basement, they found
your old flashlight,
set on a 2x4 and sealed right up. Part of the house, now.

Cancer took the old tree, too.
Galls took her branches, little by little until her crown was
nothing but knotted baubles.
They tell us you meant to let the tree burn, when it was small,

but my idealist mother marched herself down the hillside
with buckets of water
suspending disbelief for decades, thinking that saving some-
thing
means forever.

After they cut the elder down, I confided to her: *I sat with my
hands on the tree
for hours* I say, *I tried to take its disease.*

Purgatory
a poem about addiction

We used to stumble
in and
out of conversations
one
       foot
on the sidewalk crack
between planes
       of existence
sometimes
the planets
aligned for
us—others
we were two turn
signals blinking in and
out of
unison
a red light, for eternity, always
begging
for us to run it

Echo
at the Current River, Missouri

A log truck barrels towards
the old bus
ricketing us to the river,

and even our seasoned backroad driver
brakes and braces
when it whooshes by.

Shivers find his spine
as invisible, spindly fingers
graze it from the other side

Hades beckons from behind
a roadside pine
not yet acquainted with a chainsaw.

We pull up to the water's edge
to whispers
of wild horses.

Excerpt from *Underland: A Deep Time Journey*
by Robert MacFarlane

*"I have for some time now been haunted by the Saami
vision of the underland as a perfect inversion of the
human realm, with the ground always the mirror-line,
such that the 'feet of the dead, who must walk upside
down, touch those of the living, who stand upright.' The
intimacy of that posture is moving to me—the dead and
the living standing sole to sole. Seeing photographs of the
early hand-marks left on the cave walls of Maltravieso,
Lascaux or Sulawesi, I imaging laying my own palm pre-
cisely against the outline left by those unknown markers. I
imagine, too, feeling a warm hand pressing through from
within the cold rock, meeting mine fingertip to fingertip
in open-handed encounter across time."*

The Other Her

I read the other day about an ancient people, who believed
our dead walk below us, upside down. And I can't stop think-
ing about her now—the Other Me. Stepping only where I
do—my Peter Pan Shadow—toes pointed in the warm glow
of my footsteps. I wake with mine uncovered in a dark room,
tuck them up under my knees and feel her mirror my move-
ments—the Other Me. The fringe divides us, a satin curtain,
sometimes our hands meet briefly and I watch for her to step
through, but she doesn't. Does she watch for me? Does she
feel our feet get tangled in the veil, sometimes?

Vessel

A ritual for processing grief—
start with 30 black rocks, and an empty vessel
carry one with you each day and
hold it when you feel the pain
of loss—impart your sadness
through your palms and
when you're done, place it into the jar
and start again tomorrow, 'til the rocks are gone
when the vessel is full—find running water
hold the jar of black rocks under

A lone crow on an oak branch, watches
when you close
the door, when you
start the car, when you
close the blinds, at night—he's
on the neighbor's roof,
on the stacked storage units you drive by

or sometimes, not a crow at all,
but a great blue heron
apparition-over-chimney
cardinal in the back yard, finch in the front
two doves, on every powerline for miles of road

they beckon quietly, never
flapping, or cawing, or singing, just
a rustle
in the shrubbery
a shadow
through the sunroof
that you follow
to the Big Tree, sit,
in steel-cold light, the moon,
full tonight, like a high-beam
on that old bird,
in the tree above you
whispering there's
much to be done

let your toes get cold
take your jar of black rocks
to the river
hold it in the current

watch the moonlit torrent
tinge with red—the days
you held so tight, it broke
the skin, and now
when the blood
washes out with the water

"A bird guide may stay with you forever or a new one may come into your life as you change and grow. In addition to a special bird guide, others may become important to us at different times… Another level of relationship with birds are the messengers that make temporary contact to bring or help us interpret information or deal with a situation."

—Sandra Kynes,
Bird Magic

The cave at Aveline's Hole, a scientifically dated cemetery in England dating back over ten thousand years

Aveline's Hole
Mendip Hills, England

How many thousands
of years did you wait here
for the Earth to claim you
back again

Did you know the moment,
inching closer
with every rain

Could you feel when stone
and bone became
a spire, entwined
together

or has your spirit long escaped this place?

Precedence

after a study in seismic noise reduction
as a result of global COVID-19 lockdowns

I've barely turned the TV on
for 2 weeks
but, I hear they're saying
seismic noise
has quieted —
human rumble, ceased

that scientists can hear the Earth
like never before

tectonic quiet, but
other energy

& seeing Grandma Josephine
in my room last night
when I couldn't sleep

how she glided, silver, astrally
from her gold frame
turned her back to me and sat,
still and stoic,
at the foot of my bed--
You can rest, child.

Kaleidoscope

Last night I dreamed they took the old blue Subaru
apart for scrap.
And when they did, they found it full
of human ribs.

I watched the mechanic reach under the bumper
and pull them out, one by one.
Each with a little flesh, still on the bone
and blood
still wet, still red
like a maraschino cherry.

"Huh," he remarked
un-remarkedly
as I stood behind him
tried to remember, running someone over
on my way there.

Fear welling up in my brain as he pulled a skull fragment
from an endless store of bones.
He held it to my face, and I peered through the empty socket,

woke trying to remember
who I am.

Portal

Three teddy bears of
various colors
are tied to a telephone pole
and the longer they rest there
the more the ribbon holding
them resembles
razor wire; it cuts
into their sides
and when it rains
they stay wet for days
and drip dirty water
onto passersby—perhaps some kind
of warning

Ornithomancy

noun: divination by observation of the flight of birds

A great bald vulture glides
up next to me in slowest motion;
from another life he turns his head,
black eyes in my passenger window,
shakes the cobwebs off his wings

The fortune teller called herself
Persephone, and me
the High Priestess
travel to the underworld,   *she said*
bring back something   *important*

So I follow the carrion bird
as the highway downward
turns

Excerpt from *The New York Times*, Oct. 20, 2019

Emmett Till Memorial Has a New Sign. This Time, It's Bulletproof.

written by Aimee Ortiz

...For decades, the spot was unmarked, but in 2008, signs detailing Emmett's harrowing journey were installed around the region...but the sign at the Tallahatchie River location was stolen and thrown into the river.

A replacement was soon marred with bullet holes.

Then came a third, which was hit with more bullets.

Now, there's a fourth sign, this one made of steel. It weighs more than 500 pounds, it's over an inch think, and, the manufacturer says, it's bulletproof...

...<Ollie> Gordon, who was raised in the same house as Emmett, remembers her cousin as a food-loving jokester who protected her like a brother would...

The sign is made out of half an inch of AR500 steel and covered in an acrylic panel that's three-quarters of an inch thick, according to the Emmett Till Memory Project. "The sign is designed to withstand a rifle round without damage," the project's site said.

Horsemen

There's a cockroach on Instagram carrying a cigarette, trying to fit it through a too-small sewer grate. The first of four. He's building a cancerous labyrinth; Pall Malls and Parliaments stacked end to end, as far as the eye can see.

A dead raccoon on the streets of Toronto is left a pile of in-memoriam—handwritten cards, candlelight vigils.

Emmett Till's Memorial has a new sign. This time it's bulletproof.

Dead starlings litter the parking garage of a high-rise apartment. They fall from nests in ceiling insulation. They are missing a dimension. A tiny beak emerges from the concrete—as if to be born again.

Highway

4-wheel drive kicks in and we rumble over bones and fur, as if it were snow packed solid by the morning commute. A hawk wing sticks out above the mass grave-road, waving a tribute to whatever was. Before this. Faint skunk perfume wafts briefly, over the smell of wet rot. Of bones becoming dust. I can feel the axels, constantly adjusting.

I cried once, years ago after hitting a rabbit—a silver ghost glinting across the night asphalt. I can still hear the soft thud.

No one should be able to destroy so easily; by accident.

Based on the Greek myth of Orpheus and Eurydice

To Orpheus

Suddenly heavy again with
the weight of living
I felt my spirit sink back home

The depths from which you thought to pull me up,
they were not pits of hell; instead
you plucked me—as if the most delicate flower
from fields of ethereal fireflies

So when I passed the gates once more
the great dog opened an eye or two
then rested her heads

Sweet Cerberus
I am no threat, I briefly danced here
last we met

These days the river rumbles distantly
young shades glint as the moonlight hits them
death, refracted in a thousand blues

and they begin to whisper of
you, you
who couldn't trust a god, or a woman

The Vulture

A few miles down, the death road flattens out. Blacktop seeps
back into vision and now, only a stray armadillo decorates
the shoulder with its glittering entrails. It's sunny as we pass
through a deep ravine, and a cold shadow coasts in from the
East. It looks large when I see it: wingspan the size of a grown
man's, flapping fervently for a moment, to meet pace with us.
He glides up the passenger side to the open window, and his
unfeathered head cranes toward me once more. Black-bead
eyes meet mine and I know him then, my carrion compan-
ion. He will guide us through.

Polaris

When you get too deep you'll need a place to come back to.
So remember the bow of the speedboat
you rode with your sister.
Like the mist still settles on your face, now.
It smells like muddy river water,
cheese flavored bugles you'd place on each finger.

If that doesn't do it, find your 4 year old bedroom—
you'd dump out your change jar, make toys from coin faces.
You'd sit with your legs out in front of you,
cover them with cold, green pennies.
Your hands smelled like metal, tasted like blood.

Or maybe it's as simple as
your last day with the old bird dog,
when she stops spinning in circles,
rests her tired head
on your knee.

The Necromancer

after the art of Tyler Thrasher

He cups a still cicada gingerly
and its brittle wings erupt in
amethyst clusters
alive, in the palm of his hand

A serpent spine turns
to a column of jewels
his chandelier, a scorpion
menacing pincers, flecked with gold

Postmodern Midas
pulls them from the underworld –
dead but beautiful
the light only emboldens them

Based on the Greek myth of Zeus and Io

After Centuries of Chewing Cud
based on actual events

Io is tired
a hundred more years gone and
she still can't get the Moo right

the herd won't have her and
the shepherds
don't take notice that she's
carved anther gospel
in the dirt

her worn hooves hurt
from all the digging
and millennia pass, when

she wanders to the nearest edge of Earth
and hurls herself into
eternity, and the roof
of an old Volkswagen
and the countryside,
and the gods' white heifer,
both run red with blood.

The Heron

In the heart of the Styx, there's a deep blue eddy
still as heavy air before the hail.
Balanced in the silence, stands
Ardea Herodias—frozen, waiting.
The fish here hide, in
schools of glinting spirits –
the ones who missed the boatride
make their own way here, forever.
When his quick beak breaks
the surface tension,
they marble the water
with ghostly whirls –
and small, swimming morsels spin into
the eye of their storm.
He picks one off
and from its scales, drip
clouds of haunted river.

The Piasa Bird, Alton IL

Piasa

Mural of the Piasa Bird, Alton, IL

We drove a red Miata past the Piasa,
when I was eleven
watched over the river, scanned the cliff face
for the great Man Eater
Just a glimpse of feather from some cave mouth
was enough, but
before I could find him, heard thunder
above us, and raindrops fell through
the convertible top

The Vulture, Part II

His black shape, huddled
on the center line
he rustles
as the cars go by, but
shakes his head and
takes flight when I
stop the Old Blue Subaru
in awe of him—
he rises back
among the branches
shadow, all the way
home

First Will and Testament

To Earth I leave dead dinosaurs—their feathers ignite in the atmosphere, so later, men will draw them with leathery skin.

To the other Gods, I leave the artists. They'll make you a mountain, a river, Elysian fields you can lie in forever. Even after they don't believe in you anymore.

The Universe—please take the moon, and Mercury with all her flaws, the Milky Way, and dippers big and little on the stark nights in the country. I leave you the wind and the feeling of falling.

Mother Willow, have all 4 seasons. Keep the leaves that fall, they'll make you taller one day. I leave you the lost souls who'll read in your shadow, the ones who weep like you do.

And Dearest Eve, I will my strength to Women. May you never need it. May you speak and be heard. May your ribs be unbroken.

Castle of the White Giants
Natural Bridge Caverns, New Braunfels TX

Descent into warm darkness
where castles are formed
by continuous drips

they sparkle a little
in manmade lights
answering a version of the human question

if the Earth builds a fortress
damp, dark, below us
does it glitter, still?

In my mind the lights go down,
and the Ghost King rises from his Great Throne,
stretches his great arms after a long slumber

he grazes the stalagmite chandelier
with the tips of his fingers
and it chimes like Swarovski

100 ft. stone jellyfish
translucent in the cave-dark
stand fixed, perpetual, above him

and somehow, in the cold dirt
on the way down to these caverns
a green fern lives, on a speck of sun

Ardea Alba
(Great Egret)

She rides the backs of alligators,
or the weathered haunches
of the last white rhino,
tail feathers swaying with every step

she suns on the leather of his giant shoulders
glides over everglades
legs stick-straight
beats her great wings only once

the air in this world carries her,
an omen in the reservoir,
on a jet stream from the blue beyond

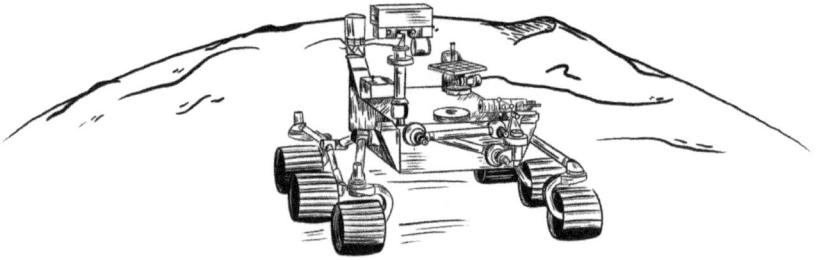

The Mars Rover, Opportunity

Oppy

for the Mars Rover, Opportunity

Such a winning way to die—
your mission, like mine, I guess
keep going until you don't anymore.

Do you ever wonder anything
like what the fuck
       am I doing here?
Is it cold? Do you even know?
Do you feel
      as alone
            as you are?
Or are the voices enough…
Oppy… they call out,
quieter every day
the call signs don't change, but
you're starting to speak
like the red dirt, now.
Will you rust on Mars?
Do your bones hurt
like mine, do
we belong here?

Necropolis

I wandered the obituaries
searching for
plot numbers,
yearned a little for
days when stone cities rose
with dead
names etched across them

Instead I found the park bench
of your memory,
where children clambered over top
of your name, to their mothers
and I wondered
if it would offend them, had I said
excuse me but
do you mind if I sit here?

Keepers

I drive to the bluffside to look for a poem
open the hatch and sit on the tailgate –
read until it gets so cold that I can't feel
my fingers, anymore

The crickets, hardly audible above the tanks
of river water—I wonder if motors are
mixing the pesticides in

I close the hatch and see my hand
outlined in gravel
dust, as if red ochre—a reminder
I was here

On the way back where I came from
a great cloud is rising—
it floats down the road like a ghost
from below us

A search and rescue team arrives
to look for this poem
and the man they find survives

Familiar

My sister sees the black cat from our childhood
on the ivy-covered hillside of our parents' home.
It turns around to look at her
and vanishes
into the overgrowth.

I remember her with one white paw –
it seems these last few lives have earned her
3 more, and a bright star in between
her yellow eyes.

We used to bring her cans of chicken
ask if she could stay, to get her vaccinations and
our parents gave half-answers while she disappeared
to some wild hideout, weeks at a time.

I know he kicked her once—the neighbor boy
she didn't come around for months, and
we never trusted him anymore

She dropped a bleeding baby mole
at our feet one day—tiny, furry,
body writhing, it wasn't dead
yet

When we fled to the treehouse, screaming
she followed us loyally

offered her prize once more at the playhouse—
doorstep stained with memories.

My sister sees a specter, from a lifetime ago
on the ivy-covered hillside, where
the house in the old tree is gone now,
but the cat's come home.

"It's no wonder then, that for centuries humans from cultures around the world such as Mesopotamia, Sumer, ancient Egypt, China, Japan, Celtic nations, and more have, subconsciously or otherwise, felt drawn to birds and viewed them as messengers or representatives of some kind of mystical communication"

—Arin Murphy-Hiscock,
The Hidden Meaning of Birds,
a Spiritual Field Guide

Les Bourgeois Vineyards on the Missouri River, Rocheport, MO

Dusk at the A-Frame

The high Missouri becomes the sky
as the sun sinks under the river

lightning bugs ascend from the understory
blinking wishes into evening

wires from the fairy lights strung above us
flicker up and hum

and stars fade in over moonlit Big Muddy
just before the satellites come on